２３４俳句
234 Haiku

ブラックカード
Black Card
Tarjeta negra

夏石番矢
Ban'ya Natsuishi

英訳　夏石番矢　エリック・セランド
スペイン語訳　エミリオ・マシア

English translations by Ban'ya Natsuishi & Eric Selland
Spanish translations by Emilio Masiá

Traducción Inglesa de Ban'ya Natsuishi y Eric Selland
Traducción Castellana de Emilio Masiá

2013

ISBN 978-81-8253-419-3

First Edition: 2013

Rs. 300/-

Cyberwit.net

HIG 45 Kaushambi Kunj, Kalindipuram

Allahabad - 211011 (U.P.) India

http://www.cyberwit.net

Tel: +(91) 9415091004 +(91) (532) 2552257

E-mail: info@cyberwit.net

Printed at Repro India Limited.

ジム・ケイシャン、ジャック・ガルミッツ、オルランド・ゴ
ンサレス・エステエヴァ、田村雅之（砂子屋書房、日本）、
安西佐有理へ特別の謝辞をささげる

Special thanks to Jim Kacian, Jack Galmitz, Orlando Gonzáles
Esteva& Masayuki Tamura (Sunagoya-shobo, Japan).

Un especial agradecimiento a Jim Kacian, Jack Galmitz, Orlando
Gonzáles Esteva Masayuki Tamura (Sunagoya-shobo, Japón) y
Sayuri Anzai.

夏石番矢

乾昌幸の筆名。1955 年兵庫県相生市生まれ。俳句創作と翻訳の優れた世界的推進者。1979 年東京大学教養学部フランス科学士号取得、1981 年同大学大学院で比較文学比較文化課程の修士号取得。1992 年明治大学教授となり、いまも教鞭を取る。1993 年中国吉林大学で講演、1994 年ドイツ、1995 年イタリアで俳句会議に招かれる。1996 年から 1998 年パリ第 7 大学客員研究員。1997 年「現代俳句」イベントを南仏で主催。1998 年鎌倉佐弓と、国際俳句季刊誌「吟遊」を創刊し、発行人となる。2000 年米国開催のグローバル俳句フェスティバル参加後、世界俳句協会を共同創立し、現在理事長を務める。2001 年スロヴェニアのヴィレニッツア詩祭、2003 年マケドニアのストゥルーガ詩祭に参加、さらに同年日本開催の第二回世界俳句協会大会実行委員会委員長を務める。2004 年ポルトガルのポルト・サントー詩祭に朗読招待。2005 年ブルガリア開催の第三回世界俳句協会大会と、第三回ウエリントン国際詩祭に出席し、日欧現代詩フェスティバル in 東京の国際俳句セッションを主催。2006 年にはリトアニア・ヴィルニュスの「詩の春」に招かれ、マケドニア開催のオフリッド・ペンクラブ会議に参加。2007 年内モンゴル・モンゴルで俳句創作を推進し、東京開催の第 4 回世界俳句協会大会実行委員会委員長。2008 年ラトヴィア、エストニア、リトアニア、イタリアの詩祭に参加ののち、東京ポエトリー・フェス

ティバル 2008 をディレクターとして開催する。2009 年フィンラン
ドのラフティ国際作家再結合 2009 に参加し、第 20 回ドルスキニン
カイ詩の秋と第 5 回世界俳句協会大会 2009 を、リトアニアでコル
ネリウス・プラテリスと共催。2010 年ハンガリーの世界俳句フェ
スティバル・ペーチ 2010、イスラエルの第 10 回シャール国際詩祭、
2011 年コロンビアの第 21 回メデジン詩祭参加に続き、第 2 回東京
ポエトリー・フェスティバルと第 6 回世界俳句協会大会 2011 を東
京で主催。2013 年第 7 回世界俳句協会大会メデジンに出席予定。
夏石は、古典的俳句の巨匠松尾芭蕉以後、最高の俳句の巨匠。

受賞歴

1980 年「俳句評論」年間推薦作家

1981 年「俳句研究」五十句競作入選（第一位）

1984 年椎の木賞

1991 年現代俳句協会賞

2002 年 21 世紀えひめ俳句賞河東碧梧桐賞

2008 年「タージ・マハール」誌へのアズサクラ国際詩賞受賞。

主要国内出版

『猟常記』、静地社、1983 年

『俳句のポエティック』、静地社、1983 年

『メトロポリティック』、牧羊社、1985 年

『真空律』、思潮社、1986 年

『現代俳句キーワード辞典』、立風書房、1990 年

『神々のフーガ』、弘栄堂書店、1990 年

『人体オペラ』、書肆山田、1990 年

『楽浪』、書肆山田、1992 年

『天才のポエジー』、邑書林、1993 年

『巨石巨木学』、書肆山田、1995 年

『俳句　百年の問い』（編著）、講談社、1995 年

『現代俳句マニュアル』、立風書房、1996 年

『俳句は友だち』、教育出版、1997 年

『地球巡礼』、立風書房、1998 年

『吟遊俳句 2000』（編著）、吟遊社、2000 年

『夏石番矢全句集　越境紀行』（初期句集『うなる川』と句集『漂流』所収）、沖積舎、2001 年

『ちびまる子ちゃんの俳句教室』、集英社、2002 年

『世界俳句入門』、沖積舎、2003 年

『世界俳句 2005　第 1 号』（編著）、西田書店、2004 年

『世界俳句 2006　第 2 号』（編著）、七月堂、2005 年

『右目の白夜』、沖積舎、2006 年

『世界俳句 2007　第 3 号』（編著）、七月堂、2007 年

『連句虚空を貫き』（カジミーロ・ド・ブリトーとの共著）、七月堂、2007 年

『展望　現代の詩歌』第 10 巻（共著）、明治書院、2007 年

『世界俳句 2008　第 4 号』（編著）、七月堂、2008 年

『空飛ぶ法王　161 俳句』、こおろ社、2008 年

『世界俳句 2009　第 5 号』（編著）、七月堂、2009 年

『日曜日の随想 2008』（共著）、日本経済新聞出版社、2009 年

『迷路のヴィルニュス』、七月堂、2009 年

『世界俳句 2010　第 6 号』（編著）、七月堂、2010 年

『俳句縦横無尽』（鎌倉佐弓との共著）、沖積舎、2010 年

『世界俳句 2011　第 7 号』（編著）、七月堂、2011 年

『世界俳句協会アンソロジー2011』（編著）、七月堂、2011 年

『世界俳句 2012　第 8 号』（編著）、七月堂、2012 年

『ブラックカード』、砂子屋書房、2012 年

『世界俳句 2013　第 9 号』（編著）、七月堂、2013 年

主要海外出版

Haiku: antichi e moderni, Garzanti Editore, Italy, 1996 (co-authored).

A Future Waterfall: 100 Haiku from the Japanese, Red Moon Press, USA,

1999 & 2004.

Romanje po Zemlji, Društvo Apokalipsa, Slovenia, 2000.

Цветята на Вятьра, Matom, Bulgaria, 2001.

Poesia Sempre NÚMERO 17, Fundação Biblioteca Nacional, Brazil, Brazil, 2002 (co-authored).

Haiku: Poetry Ancient & Modern, MQP,UK, 2002 (co-authored).

Haiku: the leaves are back on the tree, Greece, 2002(co-authored).

Ombres et Lumières, LCR, Bulgaria, 2003 (co-authored).

Haiku: Poésie anciennes et Modernes, Édition Vega, France, 2003 (co-authored).

Странный Ветер, Иностранка, Russia, 2003 (co-authored).

The Road: world haiku, Ango Boy, Bulgaria, 2004 (co-authored).

Ribnik tišine: slovenska haiku antologija, Društvo Apokalipsa, Slovenia, 2005(co-authored).

L'Anthologie du Poème Bref, Les Dossiers d'Aquitaine, France, 2005 (co-authored).

Right Eye in Twilight, Wasteland Press, USA, 2006.

ÎMBRĂȚIȘAREA PLANETELOR (THE EMBRACE OF PLANETS), Edidura Făt-Frumos, Romania, 2006.

Endless Helix: Haiku and Short Poems, Cyberwit.net, India, 2007 & 2009.

*Le bleu du martin pêcheur: Haïkus,*L'iroli, Beauvais, France,2007 (co-authored).

Madarak / Birds / 鳥*: 50 Haiku,* Balassi Kiadó, Hungary, 2007.

Pellegrinaggio terrestre / Earth Pilgrimage /地球巡礼, Albalibri Editore, Italy, 2007.

Flying Pope: 127 Haiku/空飛ぶ法王　127 俳句, Cyberwit.net, India, 2008.

Balsis no mākoņiem / Voices from the Clouds / 雲から声,Minerva, Latvia, 2008.

MUNDUS poesie per un'etica del rifiuto, Valtrend Editore Napoli, Italy, 2008(co-authored).

ŐSI FENYŐ, tr. by Vihar Judit, Napkút Kiadó, Budapest, Hungary, 2008 (co-authored).

KONCENTRIČNI KRUGOVI, PUNTA, Serbia, 2009 .

Music of the Twentieth Century, A. P. F. Publisher, USA, 2010 (co-authored).

Hybrid Paradise / ハイブリッド天国, Cyberwit.net, India, 2010.

Il Papa che vola: 44 haiku / 空飛ぶ法王　44 俳句, Rupe Mutevole, Italy, 2010.

The Individual Voice 16, Helicon Poetry Society, Israel, Tel-Aviv, Israel, 2011(co-authored).

Turquoise Milk: Selected Haiku of Ban'ya Natsuishi /ターコイズ・ミルク 夏石番矢選句集, Red Moon Press, USA, 2011.

A TENGER VILÁGA / *The World of the Sea* / 海の世界 50 HAIKU, Balassi

Kiadó, Hungary, 2012.

L'Archipel des séismes: Écrits du Japon après le 11 mars 2011, Editions

Philippe Picquier, 2012, France (co-authored).

Japanese Modern Haiku, Cyberwit.net, India, 2012 (co-authored with

Sayumi Kamakura).

LA VILLE: HAÏKU Anthologie bilingue de poètes bulgares, français et

francophones, Фаparo, 2012, Bulgaria (co-authored).

Kamesan's World Haiku Anthology on War, Violence and Human Rights

Violation, Kamesan Books, 2012, USA (co-authored).

Ban'ya Natsuishi

which is the penname of Masayuki Inui, was born in Aioi City, Hyôgo Prefecture, Japan in 1955. Prominent as an international promoterof haiku writing and translation. He studied at Tokyo University where he received a master degree in Comparative Literature and Culture in 1981. In 1992 he was appointed Professor at Meiji University where he continues to teach. In 1993 he gave lectures at Jilin University in China, he was invited to haiku meeting in 1994 in Germany, in 1995 in Italy. From 1996 to 1998 a guest research fellow at Paris 7th University. In 1997 he held "Contemporary Haiku" event in Provence of France. In 1998 with Sayumi Kamakura, he founded international haiku quarterly "Ginyu", became its Publisher and Editor-in-Chief. In 2000, after attendance to Global Haiku Festival in USA, he co-founded the World Haiku Association, in Slovenia. Currently works as the association's Director. In 2001 attended to Vilenica Poetry Festival in Slovenia, in 2003 to Struga Poetry Evenings in Macedonia, in the same year worked as the Chairman of The Steering Committee for the 2nd World Haiku Association Conference which was held in Japan. In 2004 he was invited to Poetry at Porto Santo in Portugal. In 2005 he attended to the 3rd World Haiku Association Conference in Bulgaria, the 3rd Wellington International Poetry Festival and presided international haiku session of Euro-Japan Poetry Festival in Tokyo. In 2006 he was invited to Poetry Spring in Vilnius of Lithuania and Ohrid P.E.N. Conference in Macedonia. In 2007 he visited Inner Mongolia and Mongolia to promote haiku writing there and held the 4th World Haiku Association Conference in Tokyo as its Chair. In 2008, after attendance to poetry festivals in Latvia, Estonia, Lithuania & Italy, he inaugurated Tokyo Poetry Festival 2008 as its Director. In 2009 after attendance to Lahti International Writers' Reunion 2009 in Finland, he co-organized Druskininkai Poetic Fall & the 5th World Haiku Association Conference 2009 in Lithuania with Kornelijus Platelis. In 2010 he attended to World Haiku Festival Pecs 2010 in Hungary and the 10th Sha'ar International Poetry Festival 2010 in Israel. In 2011, after attended to the 21st Medellin Poetry Festival in Colombia, he held the 2nd Tokyo Poetry Festival & the 6th World Haiku Association Conference 2011 in Tokyo, as its Director. In 2013 he will attend to the 7th World Haiku Association Conference Medellin. Natsuishi is the greatest haiku master after classic haiku master Basho Matsuo.

Among his awards are: in 1980 he was recommended as Poet of the Year by *Haiku-hyôron*, in 1981 he won First Prize in a competition sponsored by haiku monthly *Haiku-kenkyû,* in 1984 the Shii-no-ki Prize, in 1991 the Modern Haiku Association Prize, in 2002 the Hekigodô Kawahigashi Prize of the 21st Century Ehime Haiku Prize, in 2008 AZsacra International Poetry Award for *Taj Mahal Review.*

Main Japanese publication:

The Diary of Everyday Hunting (Ryôjô-ki), Seichi-sha, 1983.

Poetics of Haiku, Seichi-sha, 1983.

Métropolitique, Bokuyô-sha, 1985.

Rhythm in the Vacuum (Shinkû-ritsu), Shichô-sha, 1986.

Dictionary of Keywords for Contemporary Haiku, Rippu-shobô, 1990.

The Fugue of Gods(Kamigami no Fûga), Kôeidô-shoten, 1990.

Opera in the Human Body (Jintai Opera), Shoshi-yamada, 1990.

Waves of Joy (Rakurô), Shoshi-yamada, 1992.

Poetic Spirit of Genius, Yûshorin, 1993.

The Science of Megaliths and Big Trees (Kyoseki Kyoboku Gaku), Shoshi-yamada, 1995.

Haiku: A Century's Quest , Kôdansha, 1995 (edited).

Contemporary Haiku Manuel, Rippu-shobô, 1996.

Haiku Is Our Friend, Kyôiku-shuppan, 1997.

Earth Pilgrimage (Chikyû Junrei), Rippu-shobô, 1998.

Haiku Troubadours 2000, Ginyu Press, 2000 (edited).

Collected Haiku Poems by Ban'ya Natsuishi: Crossing Borders (Collected Early Haiku: Roaring River and *Drifting* included in this publication)*, Chûseki-sha, 2001.

Chibimaruko-chan's Haiku Class Room, Shûei-sha, 2002 (edited).

A Guide to World Haiku, Chûseki-sha, 2003.

World Haiku 2005: No. 1, Nishida-shoten, 2004 (edited).

World Haiku 2006: No. 2, Shichigatsudo, 2005 (edited).

Right Eye in Twilight (Migime no Byakuya), Chûseki-sha, 2006.

World Haiku 2007: No. 3, Shichigatsudo, 2007 (edited).

Renku: A través do ar / Through the Air/A travers l'air, Shichigatsudo, 2007 (co-authored with Casimiro de Brito).

Tenbô Gendai no Shiika Vol. 10, Meiji-shoin, 2007 (co-authored).

World Haiku 2008: No. 4, Shichigatsudo, 2008 (edited).

Flying Pope: 161 Haiku, Koorosha, 2008.

World Haiku 2009: No. 5, Shichigatsudo, 2009 (edited).

Nichiyôbi no Zuisô 2008, Nihon-keizai-shinbun-shuppansha, 2009 (co-authored).

Labyrinth of Vilnius, Shichigatsudo, 2009.

World Haiku 2010: No. 6, Shichigatsudo, 2010 (edited).

Haiku Jûômujin, Chûseki-sha, 2010 (co-authored with Sayumi Kamakura).

World Haiku 2011: No. 7, Shichigatsudo, 2011 (edited).

World Haiku Association Anthology 2011, Shichigatsudo, 2011 (edited).

World Haiku 2012: No. 8, Shichigatsudo, 2012 (edited).

Black Card, Sunagoya-shobo, 2012.

World Haiku 2013: No. 9, Shichigatsudo, 2013 (edited).

Main Overseas publication:

Haiku: antichi e moderni, Garzanti Editore, Italy, 1996 (co-authored).

A Future Waterfall: 100 Haiku from the Japanese, Red Moon Press, USA, 1999 & 2004.

Romanje po Zemlji, Društvo Apokalipsa, Slovenia, 2000.

Цветята на Вятьра, Matom, Bulgaria, 2001.

Poesia Sempre NÚMERO 17, Fundação Biblioteca Nacional, Brazil, Brazil, 2002 (co-authored).

Haiku: Poetry Ancient & Modern, MQP,UK, 2002 (co-authored).

Haiku: the leaves are back on the tree, Greece, 2002(co-authored).

Ombres et Lumières, LCR, Bulgaria, 2003 (co-authored).

Haiku: Poésie anciennes et Modernes, Édition Vega, France, 2003 (co-authored).

Странный Ветер, Иностранка, Russia, 2003 (co-authored).

The Road: world haiku, Ango Boy, Bulgaria, 2004 (co-authored).

Ribnik tišine: slovenska haiku antologija, Društvo Apokalipsa, Slovenia, 2005 (co-authored).

L'Anthologie du Poème Bref, Les Dossiers d'Aquitaine, France, 2005 (co-authored).

Right Eye in Twilight, Wasteland Press, USA, 2006.

ÎMBRĂŢIŞAREA PLANETELOR (THE EMBRACE OF PLANETS), Edidura Făt-Frumos, Romania, 2006.

Endless Helix: Haiku and Short Poems, Cyberwit.net, India, 2007 & 2009.

Le bleu du martin pêcheur: Haïkus, L'iroli, Beauvais, France, 2007 (co-authored).

MADARAK / *Birds* / 鳥: *50* HAIKU, Balassi Kiadó, Hungary, 2007.

Pellegrinaggio terrestre / Earth Pilgrimage / 地球巡礼, Albalibri Editore, Italy, 2007.

Flying Pope: 127 Haiku / 空飛ぶ法王　127 俳句, Cyberwit.net, India, 2008.

Balsis no mākoņiem / Voices from the Clouds / 雲から声, Minerva, Latvia, 2008.

MUNDUS poesie per un'etica del rifiuto, Valtrend Editore Napoli, Italy, 2008 (co-authored).

ŐSI FENYŐ, tr. by Vihar Judit, Napkút Kiadó, Budapest, Hungary, 2008 (co-authored).

KONCENTRIČNI KRUGOVI, PUNTA, Serbia, 2009.

Music of the Twentieth Century, A. P. F. Publisher, USA, 2010 (co-authored).

Hybrid Paradise / ハイブリッド天国, Cyberwit.net, India, 2010.

Il Papa che vola: 44 haiku / 空飛ぶ法王　44 俳句, Rupe Mutevole, Italy, 2010.

The Individual Voice 16, Helicon Poetry Society, Israel, Tel-Aviv, Israel, 2011(co-authored).

*Turquoise Milk: Selected Haiku of Ban'ya Natsuishi /*ターコイズ・ミルク夏石番矢選句集, Red Moon Press, USA, 2011.

A TENGER VILÁGA / *The World of the Sea* / 海の世界 50 HAIKU, Balassi Kiadó, Hungary, 2012.

L'Archipel des séismes: Écrits du Japon après le 11 mars 2011, Editions Philippe Picquier, 2012, France (co-authored).

Japanese Modern Haiku, Cyberwit.net, India, 2012 (co-authored with Sayumi Kamakura).

LA VILLE: HAÏKU Anthologie bilingue de poètes bulgares, français et francophones, Фаparo, 2012, Bulgaria (co-authored).

Kamesan's World Haiku Anthology on War, Violence and Human Rights Violation, Kamesan Books, 2012, USA (co-authored).

Ban'ya Natsuishi

Es el pseudónimo de Masayuki Inui, nacido en Aioi, Prefectura de Hyôgo, Japón, en 1955. Destacado promotor internacional de la escritura y traducción de haiku. Estudió en la Universidad de Tokio donde obtuvo la Licenciatura como M.A. (Master) en Literatura y Cultura Comparada en 1981. En 1992 obtuvo una plaza de profesor en la Universidad Meiji donde actualmente sigue ejerciendo la docencia. En 1993 dictó clases en la Universidad Jilin en China, fue invitado a un congreso de haiku en Alemania, en 1994, y en Italia, en 1995. Entre 1996 y 1998 fue miembro invitado investigador en la 7ª Universidad de Paris. En 1997 organizó el evento "Haiku Contemporáneo" en Provenza, Francia. En 1998, junto con Sayumi Kamakura, fundó la revista cuatrimestral internacional de haiku "Ginyu", ocupándose de las tareas de redactor jefe y editor. En el 2000, tras su asistencia al Festival Global de Haiku en EE.UU., confundó la Asociación Mundial de Haiku. Actualmente trabaja como Director de la asociación. En 2001 participó en el Festival de Poesía Vilenica, en Eslovenia. En 2003 en las Noches de Poesía de Struga, en Macedonia. En el mismo año trabajó como presidente del Comité Ejecutivo de la 2ª Conferencia de la Asociación Mundial de Haiku celebrada en Japón. En 2004 fue invitado a "Poesía" en Porto Santo, en Portugal. En 2005 participó en la 3ª Conferencia de la Asociación Mundial de Haiku en Bulgaria, el Tercer Certamen Internacional de Poesía de Wellington y presidió la sesión internacional de haiku del Certamen de Poesía Euro-

Japón en Tokio. En 2006 fue invitado a *Primavera de Poesía* en Vilnius, Lituania, y a la Conferencia Ohrid P.E.N. en Macedonia. En 2007 visitó Mongolia y Mongolia interior para promover la escritura de haiku en ese país; y presidió la cuarta Conferencia de la Asociación Mundial de Haiku en Tokio. En 2008, tras su asistencia a festivales de poesía en Latvia, Estonia, Lituania e Italia, inauguró el Festival de Poesía de Tokio de 2008 como Director. En 2009 tras su asistencia a la Reunión Internacional de Escritores en Lahti, Finlandia, co-organizó el *Otoño de Poesía* Druskininkai y la 5ª Conferencia de la Asociación Mundial de Haiku 2009, en Lituania, con Kornelijus Platelis. En 2010 participa en el Festival Mundial de Haiku 2010 en Pecs, Hungría, y también en el 10º Festival Internacional de Poesía Sha`ar, en Israel. En 2011, tras asistir al Festival de Poesía Medellín, en Colombia, coordinó como Director el 2º Festival de Poesía de Tokio y la 6ª Conferencia de la Asociación Mundial de Haiku 2011 en Tokio. En 2013 participará en el la 7ª Conferencia de la Asociación Mundial de Haiku, en Medellín. Natsuishi está considerado hoy como el gran maestro de haiku desde los días del clásico Basho Matsuo.

Premios literarios obtenidos: en 1980 fue recomendado como Poeta del Año por la revista Haiku-hyôron; en 1981 ganó el Primer Premio en el certamen patronizado por la revista mensual de haiku Haiku-kenkyû; en 1984 recibe el Premio Shii-no-ki; en 1991 el Premio de la Asociación de Haiku Moderno; en 2002, el Premio Hekigodô Kawahigashi del 21 Premio de Haiku Century Ehime; en 2008, el Premio Internacional Azsacra de Poesía por la Revista Taj Mahal.

Principales publicaciones en japonés:

Diario cotidiano de un cazador (Ryôjô-ki), Seichi-sha, 1983.

Poética del Haiku, Seichi-sha, 1983.

Métropolitique, Bokuyô-sha, 1985.

Ritmo del Vacío (Shinkû-ritsu), Shichô-sha, 1986.

Diccionario de conceptos clave del Haiku Contemporáneo, Rippu-shobô, 1990.

Fuga de los dioses (Kamigami no Fûga), Kôeidô-shoten, 1990.

Ópera en el cuerpo humano (Jintai Opera), Shoshi-yamada, 1990.

Olas de alegría (Rakurô), Shoshi-yamada, 1992.

Espíritu poético del Genio, Yûshorin, 1993.

La Ciencia de los Megalitos y árboles gigantes (Kyoseki Kyoboku Gaku), Shoshi-yamada, 1995.

Haiku: una investigación centenaria , Kôdansha, 1995 (escrito y editado).

Manual de Haiku Contemporáneo, Rippu-shobô, 1996.

Nuestro amigo Haiku, Kyôiku-shuppan, 1997.

Peregrinaje por la Tierra (Chikyû Junrei), Rippu-shobô, 1998.

Trovadores Haiku 2000, Ginyu Press, 2000 (escrito y editado).

Cruzando fronteras: Antología poética de Haikus de Ban'ya Natusishi
(Selección de primeros haiku: incluye Murmullo del Río y Escorar),
Chûseki-sha, 2001.

Lecciones sobre Haiku de Chibimaruko-chan, Shûei-sha, 2002 (escrito y
editado).

Guía al Mundo del Haiku, Chûseki-sha, 2003.

Mundo Haiku 2005: No. 1, Nishida-shoten, 2004 (escrito y editado).

Mundo Haiku 2006: No. 2, Shichigatsudo, 2005 (escrito y editado).

Ojo derecho de atardecer (Migime no Byakuya), Chûseki-sha, 2006.

Mundo Haiku 2007: No. 3, Shichigatsudo, 2007 (escrito y editado).

Renku: A través do ar / Through the Air / A travers l'air [A través del aire],
Shichigatsudo, 2007 (coautor con Casimiro de Brito).

Perspectivas de poesía contemporánea (Tenbô Gendai no Shiika) Vol. 10,
Meiji-shoin, 2007 (escrito y editado).

Mundo Haiku 2008: No. 4, Shichigatsudo, 2008 (escrito y editado).

Papa Volador: 161 Haiku, Koorosha, 2008.

Mundo Haiku 2009: No. 5, Shichigatsudo, 2009 (escrito y editado).

Ensayos dominicales (Nichiyôbi no Zuisô) 2008, Nihon-keizai-shinbun-
shuppansha, 2009 (coautor).

Laberinto de Vilnius, Shichigatsudo, 2009.

Mundo Haiku 2010: No. 6, Shichigatsudo, 2010 (escrito y editado).

Haiku Jûômujin, Chûseki-sha, 2010 (coautor con Sayumi Kamakura).

Mundo Haiku 2011: No. 7, Shichigatsudo, 2011 (edited).

Mundo Haiku Association Anthology 2011, Shichigatsudo, 2011 (escrito y editado).

Mundo Haiku 2012: No. 8, Shichigatsudo, 2012 (escrito y editado).

Tarjeta negra, Sunagoya-shobo, 2012.

Mundo Haiku 2013: No. 9, Shichigatsudo, 2013 (escrito y editado).

Publicaciones Internacionales:

Haiku: antichi e moderni, Garzanti Editore, Italia, 1996 (coautor).

A Future Waterfall: 100 Haiku from the Japanese, Red Moon Press, EE.UU., 1999 & 2004.

Romanje po Zemlji, Društvo Apokalipsa, Eslovenia, 2000.

ЦветятанаВятьра, Matom, Bulgaria, 2001.

Poesia Sempre NÚMERO 17, Fundação Biblioteca Nacional, Brasil, Brasil, 2002 (coautor).

Haiku: Poetry Ancient & Modern, MQP,R.U., 2002 (coautor).

Haiku: the Leaves are Back on the Tree, Grecia, 2002(coautor).

Ombres et Lumières, LCR, Bulgaria, 2003 (coautor).

Haiku: Poésie anciennes et Modernes, Édition Vega, Francia, 2003 (coautor).

СтранныйВетер, Иностранка, Rusia, 2003 (coautor).

The Road: world haiku, Ango Boy, Bulgaria, 2004 (coautor).

Ribnik tišine: slovenska haiku antologija, Društvo Apokalipsa, Eslovenia, 2005 (coautor).

L'Anthologie du Poème Bref, Les Dossiers d'Aquitaine, Francia, 2005 (coautor).

Right Eye in Twilight, Wasteland Press, EE.UU., 2006.

ÎMBRĂŢIŞAREA PLANETELOR / THE EMBRACE OF PLANETS, Editura Făt-Frumos, Rumanía, 2006.

Endless Helix: Haiku and Short Poems, Cyberwit.net, India, 2007 & 2009.

Le bleu du martin pêcheur: Haïkus, L'iroli, Beauvais, Francia, 2007 (coautor).

MADARAK / *Birds* / 鳥: *50* HAIKU, Balassi Kiadó, Hungría, 2007.

Pellegrinaggio terrestre / Earth Pilgrimage / 地球巡礼, Albalibri Editore, Italia, 2007.

Flying Pope: 127 Haiku / 空飛ぶ法王　127 俳句, Cyberwit.net, India, 2008.

Balsis no mākoņiem / Voices from the Clouds / 雲から声, Minerva, Letonia, 2008.

MUNDUS *poesie per un'etica del rifiuto*, Valtrend Editore Napoles, Italia, 2008 (coautor).

ŐSI FENYŐ, Napkút Kiadó, Budapest, Hungría, 2008 (coautor).

KONCENTRIČNI KRUGOVI, PUNTA, Serbia, 2009.

Music of the Twentieth Century, A. P. F. Publisher, EE.UU., 2010 (coautor).

Hybrid Paradise / ハイブリッド天国, Cyberwit.net, India, 2010.

Il Papa che vola: 44 haiku / 空飛ぶ法王　44 俳句, Rupe Mutevole, Italia, 2010.

The Individual Voice 16, Helicon Poetry Society, Israel, Tel-Aviv, Israel, 2011 (coautor).

Turquoise Milk: Selected Haiku of Ban'ya Natsuishi /ターコイズ・ミルク 夏石番矢選句集, Red Moon Press, EE.UU., 2011.

A TENGER VILÁGA / *The World of the Sea*/ 海の世界 50 HAIKU, Balassi Kiadó, Hungría, 2012.

L'Archipel des séismes: Écrits du Japon après le 11 mars 2011, Éditions Philippe Picquier, Francia, 2012 (coautor).

Japanese Modern Haiku, Cyberwit.net, India, 2012 (coautor con Sayumi Kamakura).

LA VILLE: HAÏKU *Anthologie bilingue de poètes bulgares, français et francophones*, Фaparo, Bulgaria, 2012 (coautor).

Kamesan's World Haiku Anthology on War, Violence and Human Rights Violation, Kamesan Books, EE.UU., 2012 (coautor).

序文

夏石番矢の最新句集『ブラックカード』は疑いもなく私たちの心に、詩人は内的現実と外的現実に直面して成功するということを教える。これらの詩は、新千年紀の苦い真実と現実をあらわにする。死という私たちの存在の根本的な問題についての次の俳句は、この詩人の深い洞察をさらけ出す。

　　死の床の眠りに飛び込む単語

コンラッドの『闇の奥』で、私たちはカートの最後のことばがささやきであることを知っている。疑いなく、番矢は死の神秘体験を深く精査している。彼の父のおごそかな記憶に書かれた俳句は、番矢の才能の集中力ある性格を示す。

　　大きなしずかなてのひら九十三年を宿す

この俳句に、死の苦い真実を伝える番矢の鋭敏な素質を見つけることができる。

津波と原子炉についての数句は、残忍な現実をあきらかにする。

　　誰も見つめられない津波に消された人たち

Fukushima の火は牙をむき水は泣く

愚かさや海岸の怪獣へ津波

敗戦後六十六年原子炉から白い煙

これらの俳句は、番矢が、世界が原子力発電所による破局に
向かっているというメッセージを携えた、注意深い調査者、
探索者であることを示す。２０１１年日本の原発が、爆発と
出火によってゆすぶられたことを私たちは知っている。放射
性物質が放出され、あまりにもたくさんの無辜の人々が不幸
な死を迎える結果となった。私たちはアルベルト・アインシ
ュタインの次のことばを思い出すべきである。「原子の解放
された力は、私たちの思考様式以外のすべてを変化させ、し
たがって私たちは比類のない破局へと押し流されている」。

これらの俳句は、核兵器の増加に困惑する現代世界の人々に
よって十分読まれる価値がある。核の火の恐怖が、番矢の詩
的魂から出る高度に情熱的で集中力ある琴線を鳴らす。これ
らの俳句によって、番矢は傑出した現代詩人のあいだに決定
的な座を占めた。
これらの俳句を読むと、創造の力、諸感情の集中性、彼の詩
の並ぶものなき様式において、番矢が現代世界で最も偉大な

俳人であることは明白である。カール・サンドバーグの詩についての精緻な定義は、番矢の俳句集『ブラックカード』に十分に適用できる。「知られざるものと知られえないものの障壁を撃つ音節を探すのが詩である。どのように虹が作られなぜ消え去るのかを語る幽霊台本が詩である」。

彼の両親の死についての次の俳句は、最善の番矢のベールを取り去る独特の力に満ちている。次のやわらかい感動を呼ぶ俳句よりも、集中的で精妙なものは、世界の俳句でほとんど探し出せないだろう。

　　　母の訃報冷たい泥水かき回す

　　　父母亡きふるさとに帰ろうとする寒さ

　　　母の遺体の前で崩れる亡き父の靴

これらの俳句は、語彙の苦心惨憺のない簡潔さという番矢の至高の天賦の才能に満ち溢れている。番矢は、至高の天才であり、俳句詩のほとんど頂点にいる。これらの俳句において、私たちは現実の偉大な番矢に出会うというのは事実である。

俳句詩人としての番矢は、自然や季語に限定され縛られていない。番矢は巧妙にこう指摘している。「俳句は季語なしにうまく書け、5・7・5音のみならず、自由詩形でもうまく書けると信じている」。鎌倉佐弓もまた、季語を使うより感情の真剣さがより重要だと指摘している。「季語は単なることば。ことばであるかぎり、作者が伝えようとする感情は、ことば自身よりも優先されるべき。私を感動させる日本の俳句は、作者の本当の情感がことばから湧き出る俳句。俳句において最も大切なのは、どれほどほんとうの感受性が俳句に含まれるか」。『ブラックカード』に収録された俳句は、精妙であり、番矢の詩を理解するのに不可欠である。

　　　鳥の歌は俳句そらで青は泳ぐ

抄出の俳句は、俳句と「鳥の歌」との大変適切で注目すべき比較によって不滅である。この俳句を再読すると、番矢がすべての時代の最も顕著な詩人のなかに含まれるに値することがわかる。この句集『ブラックカード』のなかの俳句は、どのように番矢の直観的洞察力が働き、どのように彼の内面の知恵が彼を導いているかを適切に示してくれる。

サントシュ・クマール
サイバーウィット・ネット編集主幹

FOREWORD

The latest haiku collection BLACK CARD by Ban'ya Natsuishi leaves no doubt in our minds that the poet is successful in confronting the inner and external realities. These poems reveal the bitter truth and realities of the new millennium. The following haiku about death, the fundamental issue of our existence, reveals the poet's deep insight.

A word

enters sleep—

deathbed

In Conrad's *Heart of Darkness* we notice that Kurtz's last words are a whisper. No doubt, Ban'ya delves deeply into the mysteries of death. The haiku written in the sacred memory of his father show the intense character of Ban'ya's talent:

The palm of his hand

big, silent

in it dwells ninety-three years

In the above haiku we find Ban'ya's subtle aptness in transmitting the bitter truth of death.

Several haiku about Tsunami & Nuclear Reactor reveal the brutal reality:

People obliterated

by the tsunami

no one can look

Fukushima fire

bares its fangs

water weeping

Stupidity:

the tsunami towards

a monster on the seashore

Sixty-six years after Japan's defeat

white smoke

from a nuclear reactor

These haiku show that Ban'ya is a careful searcher, explorer with the message that the world is heading for catastrophe due to nuclear power plants. We know that in 2011 the nuclear plants in Japan were rocked by explosion and fire. The radioactive material coming out resulted in unfortunate death of so many innocent persons. We should remember these wise words of Albert Einstein: "The unleashed power of the atom has changed everything save our modes of thinking, and we thus drift toward unparalleled catastrophe."

These haiku are well worth-reading by those who are perplexed by the increasing number of nuclear weapons in the contemporary world. The horror of nuclear fire draws highly passionate and intense chords from Ban'ya's poetical soul. By these haiku Ban'ya definitely takes his place among the outstanding contemporary poets.

It is quite evident after reading these haiku that Ban'ya is in creative power, in intensity of emotions, in the incomparable style of his poetry, one of the greatest haiku poets in the modern world. Carl Sandburg's subtle definition of poetry is fully applicable to Ban'ya's collection BLACK CARD: "Poetry is a search for syllables to shoot at the barriers of the unknown and the unknowable. Poetry is a phantom script telling how rainbows are made and why they go away."

The following haiku about the death of his parents are full of unique power revealing Ban'ya at his best. Scarcely anything more intense and exquisite will be found in world haiku than the following softly moving lines:

News of my mother's death:

stirring muddy water

so cold

Coldness

of returning to my hometown

father and mother gone

My deceased father's shoes

fall apart

before my mother's corpse

These haiku are full of Ban'ya's supreme gift of simplicity devoid of labored vocabulary. Ban'ya is a supreme genius, almost at the summit of haiku poetry. The fact is that we meet the real and great Ban'ya in these haiku.

Ban'ya as a haiku poet is not confined and restricted to nature and season-word. Ban'ya aptly remarks: "I believe that haiku poem can be written well without season words, written well in free form and not only in 5-7-5 syllables". Sayumi Kamakura too points out that sincerity of emotion is more important than using season words: "Season words are still merely words. As long as they are words, then the emotions the author attempts to convey with them should take precedence over the words themselves. The Japanese haiku that has touched me are those where the author's true sentiments burst from the words. What is most important in haiku is how much true feeling is included in the poem". The haiku included in BLACK CARD are exquisite and indispensable to understand Ban'ya's poetry:

> The song of a bird: a haiku
>
> blue swimming
>
> in the sky

The above haiku is imperishable due to a very apt and remarkable comparison of haiku with 'the song of a bird'. We can see, re-reading this haiku, that Ban'ya deserves to be numbered among the most distinguished poets of all times. The haiku in this collection BLACK CARD aptly show how Ban'ya's intuitive insight works and his own inner wisdom guides him.

Santosh Kumar, Editor, Cyberwit.net

PRÓLOGO

TARJETA NEGRA, la última antología de haiku de Ban'ya Natsuishi no deja lugar a dudas de la maestría de este autor al confrontar la realidad interior con la realidad exterior. Estos poemas expresan sin ambivalencias la cruda realidad y verdad de este nuevo milenio. El siguiente haiku sobre la muerte, cuestión central en nuestra existencia, deja patente la mirada profunda de este poeta.

Palabra

que vuela

al lecho de sueño y muerte

En la obra *Heart of Darkness* (El corazón de las tinieblas) de Conrad, la últimas palabras de Kurtz nos parecen un tenue susurro. No cabe duda de que Ban'ya logra captar el misterio de la muerte. El fabuloso haiku que escribió en memoria de su padre revela su talento poético:

Su mano

apacible y grande

refleja noventa y tres años

En este haiku podemos apreciar un lenguaje preciso y sutil capaz de transmitir una dura verdad.

En Tsunami y Reactor nuclear encontramos un buena muestra de haikus que afrontan esa brutal realidad:

No poder fijar la mirada:

desaparecidas víctimas

del tsunami

El fuego de Fukushima

afila sus colmillos

el agua llora

Absurdo:

el tsunami

contra un monstruo en la costa

Sesenta y seis años

tras la derrota de Japón

humo blanco desde el reactor nuclear

En estos haikus descubrimos al poeta investigador, que explora y ahonda en un mensaje que nos advierte del giro dramático de la humanidad hacia la catástrofe nuclear. Sabemos que en 2011 una grave crisis nuclear afectóe Japón con sucesivos incendios y explosiones en una central nuclear. La consecuencia de esa radiación nuclear emitida fue la dramática pérdida de muchas vidas inocentes. Conviene recordar las sabias palabras de Albert Einstein: "El poder incontrolado del átomo ha cambiado todo excepto nuestra forma de pensar, corremos hacia una catástrofe sin precedentes."

La lectura de estos haikus es muy recommendable para todos aquellos que experimentan perplejidad ante el creciente incremento de armas nucleares en el mundo contemporáneo. Ante el horror de la crisis de la central nuclear Ban'ya, responde con versos descarnados de intensos acordes. La calidad de estos haikus sitúan a Ban'ya entre los grandes poetas contemporáneos.

Estos haikus nos dan idea de la fuerza creativa, intensidad emocional, y magistral estilo poético de Ban'ya, poeta de referencia en el panorama contemporáneo de poesía haiku. La acertada definición de poesía de Carl Sandburg sería extensible a la antología TARJETA NEGRA de Ban'ya: "La poesía es la búsqueda de sílabas para difuminar las barreras del misterio y lo desconocido. La poesía es como un texto espectral que nos hablase desde otro mundo acerca del arco iris y del por qué de su extinción.."

Los siguientes haikus escritos por Ban'ya al fallecer sus padres transmiten una fuerza única. No es fácil, hoy en día, escontrar haiku que se equiparen a estos en cuanto a intensidad y expresividad sobresalientes:

El anuncio de la muerte de la madre

agita las aguas con el lodo

en un gélido estremecimiento

¡Qué frialdad!

Retornar a la aldea natal

en la orfandad absoluta

Junto a mi madre inerte

un zapato desprendido

del padre yace

En estos versos podemos apreciar el talento de Ban'ya' para expresar con una simplicidad ajena a los artificios vanos del lenguaje. Ban'ya es un excelente poeta de haiku, en cuyos poemas sentimos vibrar un estilo poético auténtico.

Estamos ante un poeta de haiku que no limita su escritura a los parámetros de las estaciones, como nos comenta acertadamente el autor: "Considero que se puede escribir bien un haiku sin emplear palabras sobre las estaciones, podemos escribir haikus, bien y de forma libre, no sólo en sílabas 5-7-5." Sayumi Kamakura coincide en este enfoque poético más interesado en transmitir una emoción transparente no limitada por la convención estilística de referir a las estaciones: "La palabra sobre estaciones climáticas del año no son más que palabras. En tanto sobre palabra, es la emoción que el poeta trata de expresar la que debe tener preferencia sobre determinadas palabras. Los haikus japoneses que realmente me han impresionado son aquellos en que el sentimiento real del autor resuena y vibra mediante la palabra. Lo esencial en el haiku es cómo expresar el sentimiento auténtico a través del poema". Los haikus de TARJETA NEGRA son exquisitas piezas líricas, indispensables para comprender la obra poética de Ban'ya.

> El canto de un pájaro:
> haiku que nada
> en el espacio azul

Este último haiku con su estupendo símil entre el haiku y "El canto de un pájaro" nos transmite una fuerza especial. Releyendo este haiku, podemos apreciar el alto escalafón literario en que se halla la obra poética. La antología de haiku TARJETA NEGRA nos da idea de la intuición y saiduría que parece guiar como brújula interior la obra y el destino del poeta.

Santosh Kumar
Editor, Cyberwit.net

雲から雲へ

From One Cloud to Another

De nube en nube

病室に満面の笑み一度の奇跡

His whole face smiling
in a hospital room —
only this a miracle

Sonrisa total
en la clínica
milagro irrepetible

父の目は祖父の目その奥のさざなみ

My father's eyes
are my grandfather's eyes
ripples in their depths

Ojos de mi padre
ojos de mi abuelo
idéntica la arruga

なだらかな死への坂道星の歌

Singing stars

over the gently sloping road

toward death

Melódicas estrellas

suave pendiente

del morir

虚栄も死も風もよぎるここ我存在す

Vanity, death

winds passing —

here I am

Viento, muerte

y vanidad pasan,

aquí moro

雨音聞こえずひとときの死の床は五階

Sound of rain unheard —
a temporary deathbed
on the 5th floor

Mudo sonido de lluvia
y en la quinta planta
una camilla temporal de muerte

雨の夜家族のために口を動かす

A rainy night
he opens his mouth without speaking
for the family

Noche de lluvia
los labios osan
hablar a la familia

雨はやみつつ渾身の父の「はい」

The rain lets up
"Yes" said vigorously
by my father, dying

Cesa de llover
la voz grave del padre dice:
"Sí"

死の床の眠りに飛び込む単語

A word
enters sleep —
deathbed

Palabra
que vuela
al lecho de sueño y muerte

大きなしずかなてのひら九十三年を宿す

The palm of his hand

big, silent

in it dwells ninety-three years

Su mano

apacible y grande

refleja noventa y tres años

口と肛門あけっぱなしの父光る雲

My father, mouth

and anus wide open —

a shining cloud

Padre

boca y ano sin cerrar

brillante nube

風は雲を運び死の床にポンプ

Wind

carrying away clouds

a pump near the deathbed

Disipa el viento nubes

bomba extractora

en el lecho mortuorio

帯電すこの世の針とあの世の針

A needle in this world

A needle in the next world

both charged with electricity

Agujas de este mundo

agujas del más allá

ambas cargadas de electricidad

桜咲き呼吸をやめる仕事が終わる

Cherry in bloom —
the task of stopping the breath
finished

Labor concluida
cesa el aliento
florece el cerezo

猫にさそわれ雲から雲へ飛ぶ父よ

Invited by cats
my father is flying
from one cloud to another

Mi padre vuela
de nube en nube
seducido por los gatos

喪失や無限の斜線は桜はなびら

Mournful loss!
A limitless slanted line:
a cherry petal

Pérdida lamentable
diagonal sin fin
flor de cerezos

風重し人と人とをへだてる煙

The wind is heavy
smoke separates
man from man

Pesa el viento
traza el humo
distancia entre personas

嵐果てかくもこうごうしき小石

After a storm

this pebble

so sublime

Tras la tormenta

deslumbrantes

pequeños guijarros

怒哀楽には正解がない青空

Our feelings

have no right answer

the blue sky

No cabe en el azul del cielo

respuesta cierta

a nuestro sentir

生は死か死は生か水漏れの音

Life is death,

death is life?

Sounds of leaking water

¿Vivir es morir?

¿morir es vivir?

gota a gota suena el agua

魂の交差点では時計が消える

On the crossroad of souls

watch and clock

must disappear

En la encrucijada de las almas

los relojes

se difuminan

ガラスの蜻蛉が火の玉となり東京一巡

A glass dragonfly

becomes a ball of fire

takes a tour of Tokyo

Libélula de cristal

cual bola incendiada

revolotea por Tokio

古池を撫で去る風もわが俳句

The wind

brushing away an old pond

is one of my haiku

Mi haiku:

Brisa flotante

en el viejo estanque

この名前の嘘はまことか　声から十字架

Is it true this name is a lie?

A cross emerges

in the voice

Cruz

en la voz

¿Es cierta la mentira de este nombre?

雨は怒りの灰を海へ流しわが仮眠

Rainwater

washing ashes of anger into the sea

my nap

Entorno los ojos

llueven

cenizas de odio sobre el mar

太い骨と細い骨へと伸びる草の根

Roots of grass
reaching thick bones
and thin bones

Las raíces
de hierba atrapan
huesos esparcidos

神々のいぶきに遠く東京で微熱

Far away from gods' breathing
I have a slight fever
in Tokyo

Estado febril
en Tokio
más allá del hálito divino

発熱や沼の底なる岩盤しずか

I'm feverish —
bedrock at marsh bottom
calm

Febril,
albufera de lecho rocoso,
paz

再会を運河と花が準備する

Canals and flowers
preparing
to meet again

Canal y flores
preparan
el reencuentro

魚臭いことば

Fishy Words

Aroma salina pescados y palabras

魚臭いことば

風も人も記憶も消え去り星の音

Winds, human beings

and memories have vanished

sounds of stars

Al son de las estrellas

el viento se esfuma

personas y memorias

豚肉を食い法を笑う地下室の神

Eating pork

sneering at the law

a god in the basement

Los dioses subterráneos

comen carne de cerdo

y se mofan de la ley

魚臭いことばが空を飛ぶしあわせ

Happiness:
fishy words
flying in the sky

Felicidad:
palabras salinas
surcan en el cielo

水音に包まれ老いて手垢を残す

Wrapped in sounds of water
he gets old
to soil something by handling

Queda la suciedad de la mano
en el sonido del agua
envuelta

曇天や聞こえないのは自分の羽音

Cloudy sky —
my own fluttering
unheard

Cielo nublado
inaudible
mi aleteo

昼の私がここで消えればことばは茸

Myself at noon
if I were to vanish from here
words would be mushrooms

Si me extingo
al mediodía
serán hongos las palabras

ロボット壊れて「あんたのせいよ」と叫ぶばかり

A broken robot

does nothing but shout

"It's your fault!"

El robot roto

no deja de gritar:

-¡Es tu culpa!-

黒薔薇の日傘が開く橋は舞台

A parasol with black roses

opens on a bridge

it's a stage

Parasol

estampado de rosas negras

abre escenario sobre el puente

逃げ帰った男を女が逃げる黴の家

A woman escaping from
a man who ran back
to the moldy home

Escapa la mujer
del hombre que, tras huir,
volvió a la casa desvencijada

埃の道果て枝から垂れる長い白髪

At the end of the dusty road
long silver hair
hanging down from a branch

Al final de un camino polvoriento,
cabello blanco
colgando de una rama

泥沼へミイラを落とせば折れる親指

Dropped a mummy

into the bog

my thumb broken

Pulgar roto

momia arrojada

en el cieno

揺りかごを求めて耳に淀む時間

Searching for a cradle

time stagnates

in the ear

Evocando la cuna,

el tiempo remansa

en los oídos

駅への道ひそかに七色放つ雲

Road to the station

secretly a cloud giving off

seven colors

Camino a la estación

furtivo arco iris

entre nubes

ことばを追いかけることばへ集中豪雨

Torrential rain pours on

a word pursuing

a word

Bajo esta lluvia torrencial,

persigue

una palabra a la otra

南への欲望である埠頭たそがれる

A wharf

is the desire for the south

it darkens

Muelle

al atardecer,

sueño del sur

流されながら毛虫ははしゃぐ一葉舟

On a leaf-boat

carried downstream

hairy caterpillars making merry

Sobre hojas a la deriva

festejan

las orugas

椅子きしむ狂った雨季の狂った選挙

A chair is creaking

a crazy election

in a crazy season of rain

Chirría la silla

estación lluviosa y de elecciones

al borde de locura

泥の国虫歯に突風は届かず

Land of mud

a gust of wind

has not reached the decayed tooth

País de lodo

las ráfagas del viento

no alcanzaron el diente cariado

空虚な塔の裏には犬の糞に黴

Behind a vacant tower

mold

on dog shit

Tras una torre desierta

mota de moho

en caca de perro

この夏の逆さ金魚は別れの姿

My goldfish doing a headstand

in summer is his

farewell posture

Afrontando el verano

el pececillo dorado

se despide

水を怒らす白く豊かでたけだけしい円

A white, rich and

ferocious circle

makes water angry

Un círculo blanco, profuso

salvaje

enerva el agua

虚勢の会議に亡霊が出る汗が出る

Meeting for a false show of power

a ghost appears

beads of sweat appear

A la reunión de los falsarios

llegó un espectro

sudor frío

故郷に帰らず深夜小さな歯を失う

Not returning home

at midnight

I lose a small tooth

Sin volver a casa

a medianoche

pierdo un diente

重たくて見えない壁を撫でて寝ころぶ

Patting a wall

heavy and invisible

I lie on the floor

Repantigado

acaricio la pared

pesada e invisible

歯は消えゆく墓標ついに遭えなかった神の墓標

A tooth is a disappearing grave

a grave for a god

I did not encounter

Un diente:

tumba desvanecida

para un dios no encontrado

次々白雲の奇跡ペーチは花

Mirage after mirage

of white clouds

Pecs is a flower

Flor de Pecs:

una tras otra

nubes blancas de sueño

注　ペーチはハンガリーの都市
Note: Pecs is a city in Hungary.
Nota: Pecs es una ciudad de Hungría.

黴、草、蜻蛉、蝙蝠の次は何か猛暑の島

What next?
after mold, grass, dragonfly and bat
An island of intense heat

Isla tórrida:
moho, hierba, libélulas y murciélagos
¿qué vendrá después?

雨のソウルへ静謐運ぶ詩を運ぶ

To rainy Seoul
I bring silence
and a poem

Vengo en silencio
a Seul lluvioso
vengo con poesías

死は最終解答ではなく山脈のうしろ鳥歌う

Death is not the last answer

a bird singing

behind the mountains

La muerte

no tiene la última palabra

en la recóndita sierra gorjean los pájaros

蒸し暑いソウルで靴、金、時間を積み上げる

Piling up and up

shoes, gold and times

in sultry Seoul

Cielo bochornoso de Seul,

zapatos, dinero y tiempo

se acumulan

ライオンが降る花崗岩の都で友と再会

It rains lions and lions

in the capital of granite

I meet again a friend

En la ciudad de granito

me reencuentro con un amigo

llueven leones

不在は子宮われらは不在への旅人

Absence is a womb

we are traveling

to the next absence

La ausencia es un seno

somos viajeros

de la ausencia

泉へと地下水黙々夜の清風

Ground water silently
running to a spring
a pure night wind

Fluye hacia el manantial
un cauce subterráneo
silenciosa brisa nocturna

人々騒ぎ空き地の空き缶から腐臭

People in a tumult,
rotten odor from
an empty can on an empty lot

Muchedumbre
tierra en barbecho, lata vacía
maloliente

長蛇の列に顔という謎西へ帰る

Enigma of faces

in a long line

returning to the west

Hacía poniente

larga procesión

de rostros enigmáticos

木の実のような脳であったか森の翁

Your brain

is a nut,

the old man of the forest?

El anciano de los bosques,

¿era un cerebro

cual fruto de árbol?

死んだ魚へ死んだことばを投げかける

I throw down
a dead word
to a dead fish

Lanzo
palabras muertas
a peces muertos

津波と原子炉

Tsunami & Nuclear Reactor

Tsunami y Reactor Nuclear

まがまがしい夕日を追って逃げ出す家族

A family flees their home

following the ominous

setting sun

Una familia escapa

persiguiendo

el ominoso sol poniente

揺れは揺れを呼び虚栄のグラスが落ちる

One shaking invites another

a glass of vanity

falling down

Un temblor sigue a otro temblor

cae hecha añicos

la copa sibarita de la arrogancia

誰も見つめられない津波に消された人たち

People obliterated
by the tsunami
no one can look

No poder fijar la mirada:
desaparecidas víctimas
del tsunami

地震後の駅前不安の臨時の祭

Accidental festival of anxiety
in front of a station
after an earthquake

Trasel terremoto
frente a la estación
ansiedad en el festival extraordinario

すべてをなめる波の巨大な舌に愛なし

No love:

a giant tongue of waves

licking everything

Inmisericorde

lengua descomunal de olas

lo barre todo

極東の不夜城へ津波千年の怒り

For a nightless castle in the Far East

tsunami is the anger

of one thousand years

Lejano Oriente

castillo inexpugnable

ataca el tsunami con furia de mil años

心不全の原子炉のそばで眠ろう

Let's sleep
near a nuclear reactor
with heart failure!

¡Durmamos
junto al reactor
de los infartos!

中性子愛も歴史も通過し闇へ

A neutron
traversing love and history
towards darkness

Neutrones sumen en la oscuridad
atraviesan el amor
y la historia también

このゆるやかな大敗北へ春の雪

Spring snow

on this slow,

but great defeat

Nieve de primavera

sobre esta suave

pero descomunal derrota

Fukushima の火は牙をむき水は泣く

Fukushima fire

bares its fangs

water weeping

El fuego de Fukushima

afila sus colmillos

el agua llora

愚かさや海岸の怪獣へ津波

Stupidity:

the tsunami towards

a monster on the seashore

Absurdo:

el tsunami

contra un monstruo en la costa

敗戦後六十六年原子炉から白い煙

Sixty-six years after Japan's defeat

white smoke

from a nuclear reactor

Sesenta y seis años

tras la derrota de Japón

humo blanco desde el reactor nuclear

鹿鳴く夜のふるさとオフラインのＰＣ

An off-line PC

in my native land

where a deer whistles in the night

Un PC desconectado

de noche un ciervo gime

en mi tierra natal

見えない火が首都の鬼門に梅の花

Invisible fire in the unlucky direction

of the capital

plum blossoms

Fuego invisible

en dirección desafortunada de la capital

flores de ciruelo

自動車の滝も生み出す大津波

A giant tsunami

gives birth to

a waterfall of cars

El tsunami gigante

engendra

cascada de coches

雪降るや神々死者の数知らず

It snows

gods don't know

the number of the dead

Nieva

Ni los dioses saben

cuántas personas murieron

空き缶や放射能の煙は風まかせ

Empty can —
smoke of radioactivity
goes with the wind

Una lata vacía
humo radiactivo
al viento

海豚が田を泳ぎこの地震は何の始まり

Dolphins swim
in a rice field
what started this earthquake?

Los delfines nadan
en campos de arroz
¿Dónde empezó el terremoto?

老母を見舞えば地震後の気力湧く

Seeing my old mother in the hospital
gives me energy
after the earthquake

En el hospital
visito a mi anciana madre
me brota la energía

杉花粉と放射能飛ぶ風の街角

Windy streets
cedar pollen and radioactivity
flying over them

Viento
de polen de cedro
radioactividad soplando por las calles

原乳は畑に流され原子炉煙る

Raw milk
poured on fields
nuclear reactor smoke

Leche entera
derramada por los campos
la nuclear humea

強風や原発の底に竹の根

A violent wind —
bamboo roots
under a nuclear plant

Tormenta de viento
brotes de bambú
al pie de la planta nuclear

原子炉という鬼がいて友もいる

There is an ogre

named nuclear reactor

and friends, too

Érase una vez un ogro

llamado central nuclear

y sus amigos

軍も悪魔も避けるその場所凍結せず

Both armies and devils

stay away from that spot

not yet frozen

De este sitio

aún sin congelar

huyeron soldados y diablos

北風の Hiroshima 目の前に十字架

North wind in Hiroshima

a cross

in front of my eyes

Viento Norte

Hiroshima

cruz ante los ojos

融けた三輪車ここに飾られ君はいない

A melted tricycle

on display

but you are not here

Donde tú ya no moras

un triciclo desvencijado

decora este lugar

Hiroshima と Fukushima という烙印へ雨が降る

It rains
on brands
named Hiroshima and Fukushima

Llueve
sobre las estigmatizadas
Hiroshima y Fukushima

風吹いて制御できない熱があちこち

Wind blows
uncontrollable heat
here and there

Rachas de viento
por doquier
calor abrasante

無知の島の地表に冥府浮上する

The land of the dead

bobs up to the surface

of the Island of Ignorance

Sobre la Isla de la Ignorancia

aflora en tierra

un yermo de muerte

草の芽にプルトニウムの豊かな洗礼

Grass bud

richly baptized

by plutonium

Tallos de hierba

bautizados

de plutonio

揺すぶられ流され致死量を超える嘘

After being shaken

and washed away

a lie beyond the lethal dose

Sacudidas y borradas por las olas

más allá

de la dosis letal de la mentira

地震と津波の島に原子炉桜咲く

Nuclear reactors

on the island of earthquakes and tsunamis

cherry blossoms in full bloom

En la isla de terremotos y tsunamis

reactores nucleares

cerezos en flor

無限崩壊

Infinite Disintegration

Destrucción infinita

長い坂の上に墓石その裏に青空

A gravestone

on top of a long slope

blue sky behind it

Sobre la extensa colina

una tumba de piedra

detrás, cielo azul

魚は泳ぎながら眠る私は眠りながら泣く

Fish sleep while swimming

I'm weeping

while sleeping

Los peces duermen

nadando

yo duermo llorando

痛みは歌声を放ち雪を降らす

After crying out a song

the pain

makes it snow

Canto

arrancado del dolor

provocó la nevada

余白に太く赤いリボンを貼る一人

A man

sticking a big, red ribbon

on a blank

Un hombre pega

una gruesa cinta roja

en los márgenes

空飛ぶ色紙に泳ぐ魚もわが子ども

Fish

in flying calligraphies

are my children, too

Aun los peces que nadan en el aire

en volantes papelillos de colores

son mis hijos

遺影へ雑多な時間が集まり北斗の夜

Various times gathered

around a photo of the dead

night of the polestar

A menudo, juntos,

en torno a la foto del fallecido

se cierne la noche del nordeste

電車で二人あたたかい三日月へ

We two by train

towards a warm

crescent

Nosotros dos en tren

rumbo a la cálida

luna creciente

白壁を白くし菫を咲かせるサムライ

Whitening a wall

letting a violet bloom

a samurai

Blanquea una pared

florece una violeta

samurai

私は西へことばの鳥はなおも西へ

I towards the west
a bird of words
further towards the west

Voy hacia poniente
el ave de las palabras
también hacia poniente

北斎の三角を見抜く獄中の知恵

Imprisoned wisdom —
seeing through
Hokusai's triangle

Sabiduría del prisionero
que intuye
el triángulo de Hokusai

遺伝子揺らぎ大地は揺らぎこの宴

Our genes sway
the ground sways
this banquet

En el banquete
oscilan nuestros genes
tiembla el suelo

肉体を着る老母はかなしや雨を苦しむ

So pretty, aged mother
wearing her body
she suffers from the rain

Madre anciana
por vestimenta su cuerpo,
lluvia y dolor

ゆるやかな坂を登れば記憶の家

Climbing a gentle slope

towards the house

filled with memories

Subo suave pendiente

hacia la casa

de recuerdos inundada

濁世をほほえみ左胸に星型金箔

Smiling in the corrupt world

gold leaf like an asterisk

on his left breast

Desde el lado izquierdo de su pecho

al mundo corrupto le sonríe

una hoja dorada en asterisco

西から西へ帰る太陽　海は沈黙

From the west to the west

the sun rolls

the sea a mute silence

Sol

rumbo a Poniente

mar de absoluto silencio

明朗な風の悪魔があなたの毛穴へ

Cheerful devil

of wind entering

through your pores

Diabólica

y jovial brisa

penetró los poros de tu piel

はしゃぐ家族空では灰の翼ふくらむ

Families make merry
a wing of ash expanding
in the sky

La familia festeja animada
cenicientas alas
se extienden en el cielo

微細な死神あなたの髪に座って笑う

Sitting on your hair
a tiny god of death
smiling

Sonríe la Parca
sentada
en tus cabellos

正体不明の塵にまみれて仏壇磨く

Covered in obscure layers of dust
I'm polishing
the family Buddhist altar

Lustro
el altar budista familiar
oscuramente empolvado

人々の湿気が残る夜の駅

Only the humidity of humans
remains
a station in the night

Solo
la humedad humana
permanece en la estación nocturna

空を流れる無限崩壊の闇の群れ

Crowds of darkness
of infinite disintegration
drifting in the sky

Cielo cuajado
de oscuridad
destrucción sin fin

電気の階段疲れたいのちを家へ

Stairs of electricity
carrying lives
to their homes

Arrastrar
vida cansada hasta la casa
por eléctricas escaleras

歯が欠けた愚者が歩くよ突風の道

A fool walking

missing a tooth

on a road in gusts of wind

Camina

un bobo desdentado

por sendero de ventisca

超現実の雲を見ながら小さな家へ

Watching

surreal clouds

I'm on my way back to a tiny house

Oteando

irreales nubes

de vuelta a casa

壊れた国の壊れた PC 座右にあり

A broken PC
from a broken country
at my right side

A mi derecha
el ordenador roto
de un país roto

鞄開かず時間の滝は浮遊する

A bag not open
a waterfall of time
floating there

Un bolso sin abrir
siento flotar aquí
cascada de tiempo

馬の肛門と女の下駄が戦う湖畔

A horse's anus and a woman's clogs

fighting each other

on the lakeshore

En la orilla del lago

unos zuecos de mujer

compiten con el ano del caballo

丘のふもと砂粒ひとつ大きくなる

At the foot of a hill

a grain of sand

grows up

Al pie de la colina

crece

un grano de arena

神の複数を人類の単数が汚染する

Human singularity

pollutes

the plurality the gods

La singularidad humana

deslustra

la pluralidad divina

蟻の幸福へ胡椒のような放射能

Onto happiness of ants

radioactivity

like pepper

Radioactividad cual pimienta

amenaza la felicidad

de las hormigas

灰色直線ときには歪み人々縛る

A straight grey line,

sometimes distorted,

binds people up

Línea recta de color ceniza

a ratos torcida

la gente atada

泥水

Muddy Water

Aguas de lodo

母の訃報冷たい泥水かき回す

News of my mother's death:
stirring muddy water
so cold

El anuncio de la muerte de la madre
agita las aguas con el lodo
en un gélido estremecimiento

父母亡きふるさとに帰ろうとする寒さ

Coldness
of returning to my hometown
father and mother gone

¡Qué frialdad!
Retornar a la aldea natal
en la orfandad absoluta

母の遺体の前で崩れる亡き父の靴

My deceased father's shoes

fall apart

before my mother's corpse

Junto a mi madre inerte

un zapato desprendido

del padre yace

無灯の家に鹿鳴くふるさとを去る

Leaving my hometown

of houses without lights

and crying deer

Abandoné la patria chica

un ciervo brama

en la casa a oscuras

地震で切断された神経からメール

An email

from a nerve

severed by an earthquake

Un mail

desde los nervios rotos

por el seísmo

ギター叩かれ熱い暗黒の逆波

Burning darkness

of stormy waves

from a beaten guitar

Ardiente oscuridad

olas contracorriente

cuerdas pulsadas de guitarra

栃の実のうつろイザナミは火を産んだ

In the hollow of a horse-chestnut
the goddess Izanami
gave birth to fire

El hueco de nuez
seno de Izanami
brota el fuego

その空白は水と火の妄想の森

This emptiness:
a forest of delusion
of water and fire

Vacuidad
alucinación forestal
de agua y fuego

犬のアパートで黄金虫のキス永遠に

In a dog's apartment
the kiss of a scarab beetle
is eternal

En la caseta del perro
beso eterno
de escarabajo dorado

暖房完備の全教室にプラスチック人参ぶら下がる

Every classroom
equipped with heating
a dangling plastic carrot

Las clases con calefacción
cuelgan del techo
zanahorias de plástico

わが右耳は日本に帰らず法王と飛ぶ

Rather than returning to Japan

my right ear

flies with the pope

Sin regresar a Japón

mi oído derecho

vuela con el Papa

ある日突然歩行者の声モノクロに

One day all of a sudden

the walkers' voice

becomes monochrome

De repente un día

la voz de los peatones

se hace monocroma

星と悪魔を織り込む布でアボガド絞る

With a cloth

interwoven with stars and devils

I squeeze an avocado

Con un paño entretejido

de estrellas y diablillos

exprimo un aguacate

プリペアドの鍋にアンデスの日の出と豚のしっぽ

In a prepared pan

sunrise of the Andes

and a pig's tail

En la olla a punto:

rabo de cerdo

y amanecer en los Andes

泳ぎながら眠る魚は悲しみの花

A fish sleeping
while swimming:
a flower of sorrow

Un pez
duerme nadando
pétalos de tristeza

二重の喪中の元日をゆすぶる地震

An earthquake
shakes up a New Year's Day
of double mourning

Sacude el seísmo
la alegría de Año Nuevo
doble luto

巡礼や管深くから鬼の息

Pilgrimage:
the breath of a demon
from deep in a tube

Peregrinación
Desde el fondo de una caña
respira un diablillo

水音は底無し命の荒野は果て無し

The sound of water is bottomless
so boundless
the desert of life

El ruido de las aguas no toca fondo
El desierto de la vida
no tiene meta

独楽は深い川を見下ろす岩で踊る

A spinning-top dancing

on a rock

overlooking a deep river

Un solo de música danza

divisando desde la roca

el río profundo

新年や見えない戦争見えない傷

The New Year:

invisible war

invisible wound

Año Nuevo

guerra invisible

heridas invisibles

虚偽の国の虚偽の小箱の中で眠る

Sleeping

in a little box of falsehood

in a land of falsehood

Encerrado en caja de mentiras

de un país de mentiras

sigo durmiendo

仏は消えてほほえみ残る松林

Pine forest:

a smile remains

after Buddha's disappearance

Se esfumó el Buda

queda su sonrisa flotando

en los pinares

ブラックカードから心臓へ灰色の線

A grey line stretches

to the heart

from a black card

Desde tarjeta negra

se desliza hasta el corazón

una firma oscura

夜の港亡き母へのことばの薔薇

Night harbor:

roses of words afloat

for my dead mother

El puerto al anochecer

rosas de palabras

para mi madre sin vida

屋根の上の牛の舌にも放射能

Radioactivity

on the tongue of a cow

on the roof

Radioactividad

hasta en la lengua

de una vaca en el tejado

先進導坑から空飛ぶ法王へプルトニウム

Plutonium

from a pilot tunnel

for the Flying Pope

La tecnología punta

desde las minas

lanza plutonio al Papa viajero

天使の休暇より長いその分子の残存

Survival of this molecule

longer than

an angel's vacation

Restos de moléculas

sobrevivirán tanto tiempo

como la ausencia de un ángel

ブラックカード

Black Card

Tarjeta negra

歯は舳　放射能舞う風を噛む

My teeth are a prow
biting the wind
in it radioactivity is dancing

Mis dientes son la proa
que masca
la danza radioactiva del aire

巨大タンポポに雷雨とてもしずかな日本人

Thunderstorm
on a giant dandelion —
the silent Japanese

Rayos y truenos
sobre el gigantesco diente de león
japoneses en silencio

恋人たちが寝ころぶ竹の皮は金箔

Lovers lying

on bamboo sheaths

of gold leaf

Los novios yacen

sobre un lecho

de hojas doradas de bambú

あの熱い平面を飛ぶ球体も涙

This sphere is a teardrop

it's flying

over that hot plane

Hasta los globos son lágrimas

que vuelan

sobre esta superficie tan caliente

鏡は嵐の海へ投げられ童は眠る

A mirror thrown
into the stormy sea
a child in deep sleep

Salta al mar
hecho añicos el espejo
mientras el niño duerme

腐る時間をステンレスの管隠匿す

A stainless tube
concealing
a time in decay

La cañería inoxidable
oculta
el tiempo que se pudre

千の水滴光らせ闇をこちらへ引き込む

Making a thousand drops of water shine
I drag darkness into the room

Que titilen a millares
las gotas de agua
arrastro la oscuridad hacia mi cuarto

影富士、地震、満月は詩人を祝福す

Shadow Fuji, earthquake
and full moon
celebrate poets

El monte Fuji en sombra,
un terremoto
y la luna llena bendice al poeta

不死鳥料理もっとも古い愛を燃やす

A meal of phoenix:

burns

the oldest love

Cocinando Fénix

reaviva ansia

de inmortalidad

ジャックは地下へ降りるバイオリンの箱の底から

Jack is going down

to the underworld

through the bottom of a violin case

Jack desciende

al mundo subterráneo

desde las entrañas de un violín

おおこの地球のまだら模様は詩人たちにも

Oh this patchy pattern of earth

discovered

by poets

¡Oh!, esta tierra dibuja

una cenefa de retales

para los poetas

虚数の雨雲の下黙々と怪物と戦う

Under clouds of imaginary numbers

fighting silently

against a monster

Peleo en silencio con los monstruos

abrumado por una avalancha

de números de ficción

その仮面　猿の冥界への入口

This mask:

an entrance

into monkey's next world

Esta máscara

una entrada

a la otra vida de los monos

突然死神君の笑顔に鯰を描く

Death suddenly

draws a catfish

on your smiling face

De repente

la Parca dibuja en tu sonrisa

un pez grotesco

指令をほしいままに発する脂肪のかたまりの濡れた唇

Wet lips

made of lumps of fat

indulge in sending out orders

Con los labios húmedos

grasientos

anhelo de orden sin más

泣きながら星を追う人いつしか石柱

Weeping

a man in pursuit of a star

will become a stone pillar someday

Alguien persigue llorando

una estrella

Llegará a convertirse en piedra

巷に漫画　聖地に自然放射能

Manga in the streets
natural radioactivity
on holy ground

Manga por las calles
Radioactividad natural
en tierra sagrada

暗ければ屠殺場からエロスの声

It's so dark
voice of eros
from the slaughterhouse

Así a oscuras
desde el matadero
voces eróticas llegan

この悲しみ雲のなかのちぎれ雲

This sorrow:

a broken cloud

among clouds

Esta tristeza:

Nubes rotas

dentro de otra nube

この秋はブラックカードの雨が降る

This autumn

it rains

black cards

Este otoño

lloverán

tarjetas negras

鋏は楽器われらの罪を薔薇にする

Scissors are a musical instrument
they make our sin
a rose

Cual instrumento musical
las tijeras convierten
nuestros pecados en rosas

原子炉を見下ろす富士は赤裸

Looking down
a nuclear power plant
Mt. Fuji is stark naked

La mirada del Fuji
desolada y desnuda
al otear radioactividad

裸富士ことばの殻のなかにわれら

Naked Fuji —

within a shell of words

we are

Cual monte Fuji desnudo

nosotros encerrados

en la concha de las palabras

火の蛇消えたベトナムからの電子のいざない

Electronic invitation

from Vietnam

where fire snakes vanish

Tentación electrónica

desde Vietnam donde ya se esfumaron

serpientes de fuego

嘘の王国蛸に水菜のひととき

The kingdom of untruth

pause for a meal of octopus

with potherb mustard

Reino de la mentira

un sorbo de algas

para el pulpo

吊り下げられ忘れられた鹿革愛す

I love deerskin

suspended

and forgotten

Me gusta la piel del ciervo

colgada

en el olvido

土を食べる少女の背中は滝である

A girl eating dirt

her back

is a waterfall

La niña

masca tierra

su espalda es una catarata

蟹と蟹の距離は私とゴッホの距離

The distance between one cancer and another

equal to the distance between me

and Van Gogh

La distancia

de un cangrejo a otro

dista como yo de Van Gogh

大地震の年しめくくる靴下からのあたたかさ

Year of the great earthquake

ends

with warmth from my socks

Expira

el año del terremoto gigante

calidez desde mis calcetines

メデジンのために

For Medellin

Para Medellín

時計無き空港赤ワインは免罪符

Airport without a clock —

red wine

an indulgence

Aeropuerto sin reloj

vino tinto

con indulgencia

時計無き空港ドルは太った死神

Airport without a clock —

US dollar

fat god of Death

Aeropuerto sin reloj

dólar americano

glotona Muerte

時計無き空港しぼんだ風船が天使

Airport without a clock —

the shriveled balloon

an angel

Aeropuerto sin reloj

globo desinflado

un ángel

叫んでいる馬糞のような排気ガス

Like horse dung

exhaust gas

cries out

Como hiede

la bosta del caballo

escape de gas

石の上の時間の檻に夢を置く

I placed a dream

in a prison of time

on a stone

Pongo un sueño

en una cárcel de tiempo

sobre una piedra

路上に熟睡の男小さな点は広がらない

A man is sound asleep on the street

a tiny dot

cannot be enlarged

Un hombre duerme

profundamente sobre la calle

Imposible agrandar un punto pequeño

球体のキリストのなか向日葵とサボテン

Within the sphere of Christ

sunflower

and cactus

Dentro del Cristo del globo

girasoles

y cactus

雨のメデジン二階は詩人たちの雷雲

Rainy Medellin —

the 2nd floor

a thundercloud of poets

Lluviosa Medellín:

en el segundo piso

un nubarrón de poetas

神々から貧しさへの坂道歌は花火

On the slope

from gods to poverty

a song is fireworks

Efímera canción los fuegos

en la pendiente que va

de los dioses a la pobreza

雄牛の鼻息が突然バスの尻から

Snort of an ox

suddenly from the rear

of a bus

De repente

a la espalda del autobús

el bufido inesperado de un buey

池の上で雲の曲芸まわりではことばの奇跡

Acrobatic clouds

above the pond, around it

a miracle of words

Unas nubes acrobáticas

sobre el estanque forjan

un milagro de palabras

鳥の歌は俳句そらで青は泳ぐ

The song of a bird: a haiku

blue swimming

in the sky

El canto de un pájaro:

haiku que nada

en el espacio azul

一枚の毛布に起伏その男の一生

Ups and downs

on a blanket

all of this man's life

Pliegues

sobre una manta

altibajos en la vida de este hombre

幸福のかけら紛れる赤いゴミ箱

A piece of happiness

disappears

in a red trash can

Retazos de dicha duermen

en el rojo cajón

de la basura

歩く穴から蜂とことばやがて月夜

Bees and words

from a walking hole

soon a moonlit night

Abejas y palabras surgen

de un agujero que deambula

Noche de luna

騒音よみがえる貧困を燃やす朝よみがえる

Noise is restored

morning that burns poverty

is restored

Vuelve el ruido;

a la mañana retorna

la incineración de la pobreza

メデジンの背骨に猛毒太陽は昼寝

Deadly poison

in Medellin's spine

the sun takes a nap

Veneno letal

sobre la espalda de Medellín

el sol duerme la siesta

Todos は熱い波詩人は太陽

"Todos" is a hot wave

a poet

the sun

"Todos" es una ola de calor

un poeta

el sol

すべては速度すべては密度すべては闇

Everything is velocity

everything is density

everything is darkness

Todo es velocidad

todo es densidad

todo, oscuridad

燃える首都

Burning Capital

Capital en llamas

燃える首都

穴のあいた雲に穴のあいた時間出現す

Time filled with holes

appears

in clouds filled with holes

Aparece

un tiempo agujereado

Entre nubes agujereadas

炎熱の坂を削れば蛇が死ぬ

If they grind down the slope

of blazing heat

a snake will die

Si allanan la cuesta ardiente

morirán

las serpientes

イエスの痕跡もないイスラエルで裸足

My bare feet

in Israel

without any trace of Jesus

Los pies desnudos en Israel

sin la más mínima huella

de Jesús

怪物か母か地中海が洗う岩

Is it a monster or our mother?

A rock brushed

by the Mediterranean

¿Es un monstruo o es la madre?

una roca alisada

por el Mediterráneo

虹の言語で俳句を書くべしガリラヤ湖

Haiku must be written

in rainbow language

the Sea of Galilee

Mar de Galilea

hay que escribir haiku

en el lenguaje del arco iris

詩人はサングラスを掏られる聖墳墓教会

A poet had his sunglasses

stolen

in the Church of the Holy Sepulchre

A un poeta le roban

las gafas de sol

en el Santo Sepulcro

雲から来た魚もあらずイエスのテーブル

No fish from clouds

on the table

of Jesus

En la mesa de Jesús

no vienen

peces desde las nubes

イエスが裸足で歩いた湖畔へ法王墜落

The Pope crashed

into the lake bank

where Jesus walked with bare feet

El Papa tropieza y cae

en la playa donde Jesús

caminó con pies desnudos

海辺の劇場イエスに出会うような再会

Theater on the seashore:

a reunion of friends

as an encounter with Jesus

Escena en la playa

reunión de amigos

como encuentro con Jesús

右耳はイエスの故郷で眠ったまま

My right ear

left sleeping

in the homeland of Jesus

Mi oido derecho

se quedó dormido

en la patria chica de Jesús

燃える首都岩と岩には愛などない

Burning capital:

no love between

a rock and a rock

Capital en llamas

no hay amor

entre roca y roca

岩でできたイエスの絶望をまた見る

Watch again

Jesus's despair

made of rocks

Contemplo de nuevo

la desesperación de Jesús

hecha de rocas

欲望の岩へ吸い寄せられては血を流す

We bleed
each time attracted by
a rock of desire

Derramo sangre
atraído una y otra vez
por la roca del deseo

夢で叫ぶ蜥蜴と風と女に叫ぶ

Crying in a dream
crying against a lizard, a wind
and a woman

Gritando en sueños
grito a la mujer,
al viento y al lagarto

わが耳と月に欠損それもまたよし

It's all right!
A defect in the moon
and my ear

Le falta un pedazo
a mi oreja y a la luna
pues qué bien así

別れののち七色の時間の棒が立つ

After a farewell
a seven-colored pole of time
stands up

Tras una despedida
un hito marca el tiempo
en siete colores

ナイジェリアの電気

Nigerian Electricity

Electricidad en Nigeria

サハラが砂のおしろい飛ばすクリスマス

The Sahara disperses its sand
as face powder
Christmas

Navidad
maquillaje de arena
dispersa el Sáhara

大使は自問す「電気と山羊と幸福とは？」

The Ambassador talking to himself:
what are electricity, goats
and happiness?

El embajador se pregunta:
¿Qué es la electricidad,
los carneros y la felicidad?

砂漠で売られるアルミの扉を電気が照らす

Electricity shines

on a door of aluminum

sold in a desert

Brilla la electricidad

en puertas de aluminio

que se venden en el desierto

竹葺きの小屋を電気は素通りす

Electricity passed by

a hut with a bamboo-covered roof

without dropping in

La electricidad pasó de puntillas

sin rozar el tejado

de la choza de bambú

針の束か大統領の砂嵐

Is it a bundle of needles?

The sandstorm

of the President

¿Es un manojo de agujas?

tormenta del desierto

del Presidente

ヘリコプターが棘人間を作るオアシス

A helicopter

makes a man of thorns

Oasis

Helicóptero en tierra

tatúa en el hombre del oasis

un mapa de espinas

電気と神とどちらが重い泥の村

Which is heavier?
Electricity or gods
in a village of mud

¿Qué pesa más,
la electricidad o los dioses,
en la aldea lodazal?

日本の鉄柱ナイジェリアのコンクリ柱結婚す

A Japanese steel pillar
and a Nigerian concrete pillar
just married

Aceros japoneses
Cementos de Nigeria
recién casados

ひざまずく電気へ神へ州知事へ

They kneel in prayer

before electricity, gods

and the governor

Todo el mundo arrodillado

ante los dioses,

la electricidad y el gobernador

北の国境電気を祝う祭に札束

Northern border —

a festival honors electricity

with wads of cash

En la frontera del norte

homenajean a la electricidad

despilfarrando billetes

数字の呪文を電力鉄鋼大臣歌う

The Minister of Electricity and Steel

singing

an incantation of numbers

El Ministro de Industria

desgrana un maleficio

de estadísticas oficiales

裸電球たちまち異人へ子供の洪水

A raw light bulb —

immediately a flood of children

around a stranger

Bombillas de luz desnudas

una oleada de niños

inunda al extranjero

泥の壁電気が不眠にさせる村

Wall of mud —
electricity plunges a village
into insomnia

Muro de barro
la electricidad
deja insomne la aldea

大使の中指祭のあとにも枝刺さり

Even after the festival
a twig stuck in the middle finger
of the Ambassador

Aun después del festival
una espina clavada insiste
en el dedo anular del embajador

くらやみ残る砂塵のなかの泥の家

Darkness lingers

in a house of mud

in a dust storm

Tras la tormenta de polvo

la casa de barro emerge

de la tiniebla